621.44
Ott

008/405

Havana Public Library District

201 West Adams Street
Havana, Illinois 62644-1321
http://www.havana.lib.il.us
(309) 543-4701

RULES

1. Books and magazines may be kept two weeks and may be renewed once for the same period.

2. A fine of ten cents a day will be charged on each book which is not returned according to the above rule. No book will be issued to any person incurring such a fine until it has been paid.

3. All injuries to books beyond reasonable wear and all losses shall be made good to the satisfaction of the Librarian.

4. Each borrower is held responsible for all items drawn on his card and for all fines accruing on the same.

21st Century
Skills Library

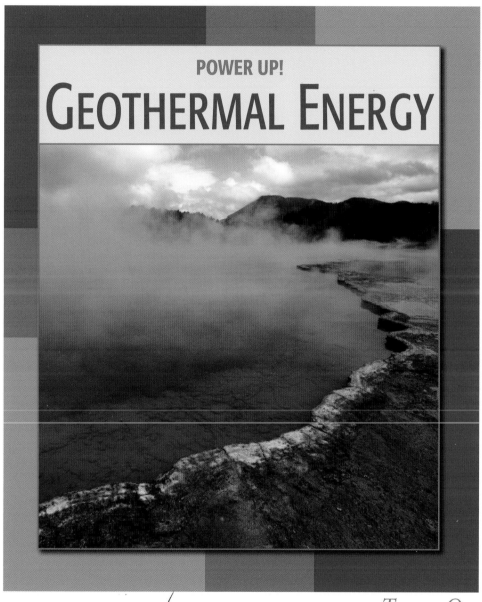

POWER UP!

GEOTHERMAL ENERGY

Tamra Orr

Cherry Lake Publishing
Ann Arbor, Michigan

Published in the United States of America by Cherry Lake Publishing
Ann Arbor, MI
www.cherrylakepublishing.com

Photo Credits: Page 11, Photo Courtesy of Library of Congress

Library of Congress Cataloging-in-Publication Data
Orr, Tamra.
  Geothermal energy/by Tamra Orr.
    p. cm.—(Power up!)
  ISBN-13: 978-1-60279-044-5 (lib. bdg.)   978-1-60279-097-1 (pbk.)
  ISBN-10: 1-60279-044-2 (lib. bdg.)   1-60279-097-3 (pbk.)
  1. Geothermal engineering—Juvenile literature. 2. Geothermal
resources—Juvenile literature. I. Title. II. Series.
  TJ280.7.O77 2008
  621.44—dc22   2007005620

*Cherry Lake Publishing would like to acknowledge the work of
The Partnership for 21st Century Skills.
Please visit www.21stcenturyskills.org for more information.*

TABLE OF CONTENTS

CHAPTER ONE

JOURNEY TO THE CENTER OF THE EARTH

The world is a very busy place. People are always hurrying on their way

to or from somewhere. Streets and highways are full of endless lines of

People worldwide, such as these in London, England, rarely think about the power that the earth below their feet contains.

traffic. Sidewalks are covered in pedestrians. Restaurants, stores, schools, and office buildings are packed.

With a population of 6.5 billion people above the Earth's surface, there is rarely a quiet moment. Believe it or not, there is just as much activity going on below the Earth's surface, too.

Peeling Back the Layers

The Earth is made up of layers similar to a hard-boiled egg. On the outside is the tough shell. This is the Earth's **crust**. It varies in thickness from as little as three miles (4.8 km) to as much as 50 miles (80.5 km).

*The Earth's crust is just the very thin surface, signified
by the narrow black outside band on this drawing.*

The next layer is like the white part of the egg. This is the **mantle**. It is made up of partially melted or **molten** rock. The temperatures here range between 1,200 and 2,280 degrees F (650 and 1,250 degrees C.)

The center of the Earth is the **core**. It is divided up into an inner solid part and a liquid outer part. The temperatures here are so hot that it is hard to even imagine them. They range between 7,000 and 12,600 degrees F (3,900 and 7,000 degrees C.) In the outer core, rocks have been turned into liquid because it is so hot. This liquid is called **magma**. It stays hot for between five thousand and a million years.

Learning & Innovation Skills

Just as happens deep in the Earth, decaying radioactive elements heat water to steam in nuclear power plants. The steam drives turbines to produce electricity. Why is this an efficient way to create electricity?

The incredibly high temperatures in the center of the Earth are due to the decay, or breaking down, of **radioactive** elements. The further you dig down into the ground, the hotter it gets. And that's not all. While it may look like these parts of the earth are just sitting there quietly, in truth they are always on the move.

CHAPTER TWO

WHEN ENERGY ERUPTS

The San Andreas Fault runs north/south through California and is so near the surface in some places that you can stand on it.

The magma deep in the center of the Earth does not stay there. Pressure

from below pushes it upwards over time. It comes up into the mantle

through cracks and thin spots. The main way that the magma is able to

move towards the surface is due to the movement of **tectonic plates**. These plates are huge pieces of a solid material that float on the Earth's interior like rafts on a pond.

Slow Collisions

As these plates move apart, the magma below them begins to rise, forming new crust. However, when the plates happen to run into each other, one is forced below the other one. The plate on the bottom slides down into the hotter regions. Magma seeps upward. If it reaches all the way to surface, it builds a volcano. The magma flows—or explodes—out of the earth. Then it is called **lava**.

When the Earth Shakes

The edges of tectonic plates are jagged. If they run into each other hard enough, they can create a *very* big jerk. Another name for this is **earthquake**. San Francisco, California, suffered a terrible earthquake on April 18, 1906. It happened at 5:12 A.M. along almost 300 miles (483 km) of the San Andreas Fault. The quake and resulting fire is believed to have led to the loss of thousands of lives.

The 1906 San Francisco earthquake left about 250,000 people—some 2/3 of the city's population—homeless.

Old Faithful is actually just one of more than 10,000 hot springs and geysers in Yellowstone National Park.

Not all magma that rises towards the surface makes it though. A lot is stuck a few miles (kilometers) underneath the Earth's crust. If this magma hits underground rainwater, it creates steam. Sometimes this steam builds up enough pressure to break through, createing geysers such as Old Faithful at Yellowstone National Park. Sometimes the pressure is not enough to create a geyser and just forms a hot spring instead.

The enormous heat found underneath the surface of the Earth is known as geothermal. "Geo" is the Greek word for *earth*. "Therme" means *heat*. The word geothermal means *earth heat*.

Geothermal heat may be the planet's best option for a source of reliable and clean energy. It is completely natural and will almost never run out. It has been a part of the world's history for billions of years.

Learning & Innovation Skills

Much of this heat becomes available near the edges of the ten tectonic plates on the Earth. How might we harness this heat energy?

CHAPTER THREE

GEOTHERMAL HEAT THROUGHOUT HISTORY

Many Roman baths had seats and steps down into the water around the outside. Some even had wall niches for drinks and snacks.

The idea of using the heat from deep inside the Earth is not a new one. In Pompeii, ancient Romans used geothermal water to heat buildings. The Romans also used the heated water to treat health problems such as eye and skin diseases. They liked to relax and take long baths in the hot springs, too. Hot springs were so important that wars were fought over lands containing them.

Ancient Native Americans built their settlements around hot springs when they could. They used the naturally heated water for cooking, warmth, and healing. They believed that the Great Spirit lived there. The waters were so sacred that warring tribes bathed there together in peace. Every major hot spring in the United States was once a site of Native American life. Today, Native Americans in New Mexico and Nevada are developing geothermal energy sites on their tribal lands.

21st Century Content

Native Americans are using their creativity to make use of the natural resource of geothermal energy. Native people in many other parts of the world also find ways to use the energy from the Earth.

Japanese geothermal baths can be outdoors or indoors. The baths come in many sizes, and most have very hot water.

In Japan, **communal** or social bathing is a tradition more than a thousand years old. The baths are more like places to relax than to get clean. The hot water often comes from underground hot springs. All bathers are careful to scrub their bodies and wash their hair *before* entering the hot water. Today, the baths continue to attract millions of visitors each year, and many of the baths have grown into modern resorts and spas.

Finding the Hot Spots

As time went on, geologists, engineers, and others

began to realize that there truly was untapped energy

just waiting below the Earth's surface! They began

searching for the "hot spots," or places with the

highest underground temperatures and the thinnest

crust. In the United States, most of the hot spots are

in California, Nevada, Arizona, Oregon, and Idaho.

Worldwide other major hot spots are in Iceland,

Japan, and New Zealand.

Experts estimate that the amount of heat within 33,000 feet (10,058 meters) of Earth's surface contains 50,000 times more energy than all of the oil and natural gas reserves in the world! One day countries that harness this energy may share it as Saudi Arabia, Mexico, and other oil-producing nations share their resources.

Two Power Stations

The ancient Romans used the geothermal waters in the Tuscany region of Italy for bathing. Today, it is the site of the Larderello Power Station, the world's first geothermal power station. It opened in 1904 and is still in use.

The world's second geothermal power plant was built in Wairekei, New Zealand, in 1958. It is also still active today and provides more than four percent of New Zealand's electricity.

Iceland is a modern island nation in the northern

Atlantic Ocean. People have lived there for more

than 1,200 years. During much of that time, they

have used the geothermal energy that is plentiful.

Today, Iceland's capital city, Reykjavik, is home to the

world's largest and most powerful geothermal power

plant. The plant generates electricity as well as hot

water. Both help keep overall energy costs low.

21st Century Content

Iceland has more hot springs than any other country in the world. Amazingly, Iceland also has glaciers! Because lava from the country's many active volcanoes continually covers the land, more than 60 percent of Iceland's land area is classified as "wasteland." To find out more about this unusual country, go to *http://www.iceland.is/*

CHAPTER FOUR

BRINGING UP THE HEAT

Geothermal energy can power electricity generation, and in cold climates geothermal can be sent directly to homes to heat them.

The deeper you drill into the Earth, the higher the temperature rises.

But how does this intense heat underground help people who live above

ground? One way is to generate electricity. Deep wells are drilled down to the hot water and heat. Next, these are piped to the surface. Their energy is used to power the generators in electrical plants. In turn, this provides electricity to homes, schools, businesses, and other places.

Geothermal energy can also be used in agriculture. For example, some farmers in Japan and the United States use the heated water in raising fish. The heated water speeds up the animals' growth. This makes it possible for farmers to get their "crops" to market sooner. Among the fish that are raised with heated water are catfish, trout, and tilapia. Japanese farmers even raise alligators this way!

Other Uses

Geothermal water can provide greenhouses with heat during winter

months. The same heat can be used to dry onions or lumber, too. The hot

water itself is sometimes used to wash raw wool and pasteurize milk.

Farmers in Colorado use geothermal wells to heat tomato
greenhouses and to water the tomatoes, too.

In Klamath Falls, Oregon, geothermal heat is piped under roads and sidewalks during the winter to keep them from freezing over. Of course, geothermal water supplies some spas and resorts around the world.

Heat Pumps

Of course, one of the most important ways that geothermal energy is used is in heat pumps. They keep people warm in the winter and cool in the summer by either removing heat from the Earth and pumping it inside or reversing the process. This option appeals to many people. By the end of 2005, more than 600,000 geothermal heat pumps had been installed in the U.S. Each year, another 50,000 to 60,000 are added.

At least 70 countries use geothermal energy. The United States' largest geothermal power station is The Geysers in California. It began as a health resort in the 1850s. Today, it creates enough power to supply all the homes in the California cities of San Francisco and Oakland.

CHAPTER FIVE

INTO THE FUTURE

*Today, the world is only beginning to make use
of available geothermal resources.*

Geothermal sources today provide less than one percent of America's energy. However, this amount of energy still equals 60 million barrels of oil a year. In addition, geothermal energy is the third largest source of renewable energy in the country, and it is growing at approximately eight percent a year. The U.S. Department of Energy wants geothermal energy to provide up to ten percent of the electricity in the western United States by 2020.

Possibilities for Today and Tomorrow

As the map shows, most geothermal resources in America are in western states. Today almost all geothermal energy production is in the state of

As geothermal energy continues to grow, people will become more and more aware of it. What are some things you can do to find out more about geothermal energy and how you might use it?

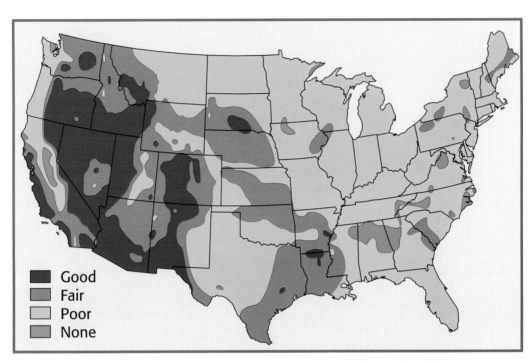

Arizona, New Mexico, California, Nevada, Colorado, Utah, Idaho, and Oregon have large geothermal energy resources.

California. There are plants near Los Angeles and north of San Francisco.

Smaller plants are found in Nevada and Utah. However, states such

as Indiana, Florida, and North Dakota are out of luck. They have few

geothermal resources to draw on.

The Positive Side

Geothermal energy is a wonderful choice in many ways, such as being an **infinite** power source. Geothermal energy is also clean because no fuels are burned to manufacture its steam power, and its plants do not need much land because they sit right on top of their fuel source. Nor can the plants create environmental disasters such as oil spills. Finally, geothermal plants are reliable and can run 24 hours a day, seven days a week.

Learning & Innovation Skills

The sun is also an infinite power source that is now becoming more widely used. You may even have a solar powered machine, such as a pocket calculator, in your home already. Why would electrical production with solar power be a better idea in San Antonio, Texas, than in London, England? *Hint:* Think about the climate.

Since geothermal energy use is still relatively rare, it is sometimes fairly expensive to build plants that use it. How might the development of more geothermal energy sources help solve this problem?

The Negative Side

However, no energy source is completely free of problems, geothermal energy included. Some **environmentalists** say that when steam is brought up from below the Earth it also brings toxic minerals. They worry that these minerals will eventually reach nearby streams, rivers, and lakes. Other people say that geothermal plants create noise pollution. The sound of pumping up the water and steam is so loud that it is often heard several miles away.

Despite a few problems, many scientists agree that geothermal energy is a positive way to create more power in the future. Certainly, as the world's population continues to grow, so will its energy needs.

The major energy sources of coal, oil, and natural gas have limitations including cost, availability, and pollution. Geothermal energy comes ready-made, right from the ground! With sufficient effort, let's all hope the issues of possible water pollution and too much noise can be solved.

More than half the population of Reykjavik, the capital of Iceland, gets its energy from geothermal plants.

GLOSSARY

communal (kuh-MYOON-l) used or shared in common with everyone in a group

core (kohr) central, innermost, portion of the Earth

crust (kruhst) outer layer of the Earth

earthquake (ERTH-kwayk) shaking of the Earth's surface, usually along fault lines

environmentalists (en-vahy-ruhn-MEN-tl-ists) experts on environmental problems

geysers (GAHY-zers) fountains of hot water that erupt periodically from the earth

infinite (IN-fuh-nit) having no boundaries or limits

lava (LAH-vuh) magma that has broken through the Earth's surface

magma (MAG-muh) partially melted rocks in the Earth's mantle

mantle (MAN-tl) middle layer of the Earth

molten (MOL-tuhn) heating of a solid substance until it melts

radioactive (rey-dee-oh-AK-tiv) material made up of atoms in which radioactivity occurs

tectonic plates (tek-TON-ik pleyts) moving plates of the earth

For More Information:

Books

Gibson, Diane. *Geothermal Power.*
Mankato, MN: Smart Apple Media, 2004.

Graham, Ian. *Energy Forever? Geothermal and Bio-Energy.*
London: Hodder and Stoughton, 2001.

Morris, Neil. *Geothermal Power.* Mankato,
MN: Smart Apple Media, 2006.

Reynoldson, Fiona. *Geothermals and Bio-Energy.*
London: Hodder Wayland, 2005.

Savage, Lorraine. *Geothermal Power.* Detroit: Greenhaven Press, 2006.

Sherman, Joseph. *Geothermal Power.*
Mankato, MN: Capstone Press, 2006.

Other Media

To find out about all kinds of energy sources,
go to *www.eia.doe.gov/kids*

For more information about heat pumps go to
www.igshpa.okstate.edu

International Geothermal Association has a useful website at
http://iga.cnr.it/index.php

School handouts on geothermal energy can be found at
www.energyforkeeps.org

A good site to find out more about the earth's mantle is
http://amos.indiana.edu/library/scripts/mantle.html

INDEX

ABOUT THE AUTHOR

Tamra Orr is a full-time writer and author living in the gorgeous Pacific Northwest. She loves her job because she learns more about the world every single day and then turns that information into pop quizzes for her patient and tolerant children (ages 16, 13, and 10). She has written more than 80 nonfiction books for people of all ages, so she never runs out of material and is sure she'd be a champion on *Jeopardy!*